AF469316

Varying Degrees of Nothingness

Thoughts, Shorts & Rhymes (of sorts)

By
Jack. C. Phillips

Illustrated by
Mila Rocha & Jack Phillips

Camelot Publishing Company
PO Box 756
Waukee, IA 50263 U.S.A.
www.camelotpublishingco.com

ISBN 978-1-944442-05-7

PUBLISHER'S NOTE: This is a work of fiction. Names, characters, places, and incidents are the product of the author's imagination or are used fictitiously, and any resemblance to actual persons, living or dead, business establishments, events, or locales is entirely coincidental.

Printed in the United States of America
and in Great Britain

To a
good man and
a better Friend
All the very best

[illegible signature]

Acknowledgements

Thanks to *J.F*, my Guru Sonam, the wandering spirit, love you bro.

To all at Camelot Publishing, particularly my ever-patient editor, Mica Rossi.

To the beautiful and extremely talented Mila Rocha for her artistry *(So what? I'm biased...),* and to my friend Martin Pachacz for his wonderful photo that I obliterated for my poem, *I.*

I also want to thank Billy, just for being a good friend, and not least of all my beloved wife, Neide Franca, for giving me time and space to work.

For my friends
Walder Rocha, Henry Tolino,
Billy Grossart and Jason Lipson

***And The Newest Little Phillips Man,
Noah***

*In Loving Memory of
Annie McIntyre*

And all the dead dears...

Life itself is only a vision. A dream.

Nothing exists, save empty space and you.

And you... are but a thought.

Mark Twain

I said to Leonard Cohen,
how lonely does it get?

Leonard Cohen hasn't answered me yet...

Foreword

In this neat, little volume I have sought to bring together a collection of short stories - some of which have inspired fully-fledged novels - the bits and pieces that are the seedlings of larger projects, a few musings and ramblings, and various attempts at poetry. The illustrations are courtesy of my multi-talented step-daughter, Mila Rocha, added to which are one or two graphic illustrations I have created myself and thrown in for good measure. The book is a collection of both juvenilia and more recent efforts, some sad, some comical, others dark and introspective, but all of which I hope you enjoy immensely.

In creating this literary offering, I endeavoured to write the kind of book you might keep in your bag and bring out occasionally to read a page or two, then put away until you next feel the need to read it. This is my favourite kind of book - the type that is sadly in too-short a supply - like a trusted old friend, always there when needed without necessarily demanding too much in return.

So here I'll take my leave. Go, open a random page and read what's there. And if that doesn't take your fancy, open another one. I guarantee there's something here for everyone.

Keep reading.

Jack. C. Phillips

Contents

Prologue

Caring I find, is the hardest part.

It's really difficult to get an interest in things when you feel so disconnected. It's almost like accepting you're dying. Like you're letting go bit by bit. The depression has lifted, thankfully, and the sadness has faded, still there, but muted like the buzz of an insect when you cover it over with a jar.

It lives with me now like an old friend and I find everything tinged with it. The birth of a baby, destined to die. Familiar places that stand frozen in time, a testament to endurance, when everything that made them special and familiar has long since gone.

Time itself the saddest concept, like it has caught up with its own tomorrow and has nowhere else to go.

'*Of time you would make a stream, upon whose banks you would sit and watch its flowing.*'

I sit today by my own personal time stream and see it is barren and without life, its banks yellow and parched, its riverbed cracked and dry.

I don't mind though. I shrug and move on, because caring, I find, is becoming increasingly difficult.

No. 41 Burlington Road

Seasons, seasons

Part One

Spring

Hush. Listen.
Listen carefully now.
Ignore the distant murmur of the lively, babbling brook.
The nervous giggle of soon-to-be-brides at their trousseau.
Ignore the sounds of excited children, let loose in park with dog and football. Each mother's plea to wrap up well unheeded, as doors slam and sentences trail off idly, as they return bosom-warm to their flower arranging, chocolate egg making, cake baking…pill taking.

Forget the chattering birds that hop demented from branch, to branch, to branch, their feathers fretted in the gentle breeze.
And the distant, tinny, penny-whistled signature tune of the ice-cream van that carries on the warm, scented spring air, thin and hollow and…

Close your ears to the lame lamb-bleating of
the newborn in the field, trying for the first
time to find his feet.
The tiny fibrous crack of that something
hatching at the bottom of your garden.
And ignore the gentle, sweeping sigh of the
young flower, turning its head for the first time
towards a half-strength sun, who'll bless that
lovely face with its warm, maternal kiss.

Listen closely now, beyond the piteous mews
of tiny helpless kittens who stumble birth-
weary and blind, fighting off weaker siblings in
their quest for mother's food.

Somewhere, amid the sounds of this, our most
prolific of seasons, if you listen closely enough
you'll hear. Though vague, once hard as iron…

The icy moan of winter's dying breath.

Reminisces

It was a kind of dirty twilight, that gloomy, introspective time of day when the temperature begins to drop but it's too early to draw the curtains against the night.
The wind had begun to howl across the common and nip at my skin, so I turned up the collar of my overcoat and sunk my hands deep into the pockets.

To be honest, I liked my cold, twilight jaunts. Nobody about, just me in my trilby hat and overcoat. I liked to pretend I was Bogart as Sam Spade, or Philip Marlow out on a case…where danger lurked in every corner. The streets were shrouded in mist, and the gaslights cast eerie shadows on the pavement. I'd find the missing diamonds, get involved in a shootout, do away with the gangsters and get double-crossed by some broad and all before the six o clock news.

Here's looking at you kid, I thought, smiling to myself.

I suddenly thought of the old cinema. I'd heard on the radio it was to be knocked down, to my great disappointment. It was an old haunt of mine and the last remaining relic of a bygone era. Probably to be replaced by some amusement arcade or nightclub. I sighed, kicking a pebble that had found itself in my path. I thought of taking the long way home, one last walk down memory lane before the bulldozers did their worst.

I could hear my dog, Ben, nose to the ground, snouting in the undergrowth and tormenting the wildlife. When I whistled, he came running back. I attached his lead and we headed off.

The cinema stood on top of the hill just before you reached town, taking the full force of the north wind. I remember it was always cold in there even in summer. My heart sank when I saw it all boarded up and forlorn. This once-beautiful art deco movie palace, with its outside ticket box, gilded pillars, velvet curtains and balcony, would soon be razed to the ground. It would disappear as though it had never been there at all.

I closed my eyes for a second and let my imagination bring back the life, the magic and the splendour of the tired old building. I could see the bright lights, hear the music in the foyer. The excited crowd in their Sunday best, buying their tickets and popcorn and the crowded auditorium with the couples cuddled up in the back row double seats.

'Of all the cinemas in all the towns in all the world, they had to knock down mine.'

I felt morose like one feels when hearing of the death of an old friend. My dog, who'd been sat patiently throughout, whined and tapped me with his paw.

'It's over Ben.' I sighed and he looked up at me with his sad, Bette Davis spaniel eyes. 'The end of an era.'

The wind howled around the condemned building and whipped at my face, and I suddenly felt more like the potential first victim in a b-rated horror than Bogart.

‘Come, boy,’ I said, and we walked away silently into the night.

White Star

Ominous against the starry
Sky, this glacial giant looms.
Portent of doom.
The gods incensed
Turn Titan against Titan.

The mighty humbled,
As treacherous jaws
Rent her fragile skin. No
Foresight could save her.
Her fate sealed, her sister

Turns a deaf ear to her cries.
Traitor in the face of adversity.
Born of chaos. Fashioned in magnificence.
Her destiny foretold.
Betrayed in the face of arrogance and greed.

Dressed in their best, the chosen few
Anticipate the impending disaster
With resigned consternation.
Still our cries turn to mist and
Are lost in the impenetrable black.

Oceanus slays his own
And then is banished.

Neptune rules these waves.
The gods have spoken and
The elements bow in their favour.

Empowering this queen
To her watery grave.
Beauty is abundance. Power
And mass. Conceit turns in on itself
And hundreds perish.

This night, black,
Moonless and silent,
Death and fear stalk these decks.
Though prejudice is not theirs,
The cook, captain and ship's cat

Will perish come dawn.
This mighty Titan, radiant still
In defeat, sinks ever lower
With portholes blazing.
Panic ensues.

Ever brave, the band plays on
Nearer My God to Thee…
Whilst below deck, in mortal
Shock, the ship's father winds clock
On mantle for the very last time.
Love's labour no more.

and the band played on...

The Weaver

The day was a peculiar shade of red, although the dawn had long since passed and the twilight hours were not yet upon us. I walked the narrow, cobbled street, home to many curious little shops and businesses – haberdashery, apothecary, candle-maker, teashop – a million miles away from the high street chains and out-of-town retail parks that had all but driven these tiny independents to extinction. It was in one such shop on Thistle Street that I hoped to finally find what I had been looking for.

The crimson-tinged, candy-floss clouds hung low that strange autumnal day, and a wispy mist was draped about the cobbled streets, winding itself about my feet and legs like an ethereal asp. A fine drizzle made everything feel miserable and sodden and soaked my exposed face and head.

Christmas was looming, and the stone-fronted, bow-windowed shops were well lit and bedecked with festive trimmings, giving the street a Dickensian feel. Through the tearoom window I could see the glow of a log fire and resolved to treat myself to a pot of Earl Grey and a toasted teacake when I had concluded my business. I was about to cross the street when a man carrying many boxes, and piled far too high to be deemed sensible, came out of one of the shop doorways and careered straight into me. He let out a cry, boxes flew and I was knocked aside, too shocked to protest or call out, and straight into the wall, there cracking my head with some force against the unyielding stone. The next thing I knew, the man with the boxes was standing over me, a look of concern on what would have been an otherwise jovial, ruddy face.

'Ye all right, pal?' he asked me in that broad Scots accent I so loved to hear. A warm smile lit up his weather-beaten face as my eyes flickered open in response. 'I didnae see ye there, ken? Over ma messages.'

'I'm fine.' I groaned, rubbing my head which appeared even as we spoke to be coming out in an enormous lump. He reached out and with shovel-like hands as red as his face, pulled me to my feet.

'I'm fine honestly, it's fine.' I grinned at him. 'I was day-dreaming and should have been watching where I was going.'

'Aye well, it pays t' be mindful these days an' keep ye wits aboot ye. There cud'a been a nasty accident there, ye ken?' And throwing his head back with a hearty chuckle, he stacked up his now crumpled boxes and left me bemused and bewildered and wondering how between us we had managed to make this all my fault.

I looked around me dazed, my vision blurred and my second head throbbing as though it contained its own pulse. I blinked and then blinked again.

The street seemed to have changed. Now it really looked like a scene from Oliver Twist. All signs of modern life – street signs, electric lights and painted yellow lines – the familiar insignia of everyday life had vanished. Flickering, foul-smelling gaslights had replaced the stark electric bulbs in the old lanterns, these casting deep shadows up and down the street, which seemed to shrink back into dank, forbidding alleyways.

The shops were different too. Outside of a butcher's shop hung rabbits and headless fowl from huge mean-looking hooks. A pig's head stared dull and lifeless from the shop window, and around the bottom of the heavy wooden door, an accumulation of sawdust, stained scarlet with blood, had collected on the slate-tiled floor. I heard a screech from the next-door shop and peered my head around to see a portly lady in a grubby cotton bonnet scolding a poor hapless lad. A fire glowed from a huge Carron range, gleaming and black-leaded. An oven door was open, the delicious smell of freshly baked pies mingling with the stench of blood and burning gas.

I looked around me, suddenly feeling very frightened. Something felt wrong, out of place…no, not quite, more, out of time. Was I suffering from concussion? Surely the blow hadn't been that bad?

I was lost! Where was I meant to be going? Wasn't there a tailor's shop here somewhere? And then I saw it, set back a little from the others in a small dip. A dark, dingy, inconspicuous shop, easy to miss at the best of times. I crossed the road and entered; the door creaked and a bell rang out a warning, an ugly croaky sound.

The shop was musty and dusty and ill-lit. Rolls of fabric obscured the window, shutting out what little light a day at the tail-end of the year could offer. A dark wooden bow-fronted counter displayed old-fashioned sewing kits, needles of varying lengths and thicknesses, mean-looking scissors and row upon row of cotton on large wooden bobbins.

An old man with half-moon spectacles stepped out from a darkened corner where he appeared to have been pinning fabric to an ancient-looking mannequin. He was finely dressed in a waistcoat and crisp white shirt. A gold Albert chain and fob threaded through a button hole and disappeared into his pocket like a curling snake. He was tiny, little more than four foot, and his hair, although sparse on top, grew thick and curly on the sides of his head, finishing at his collar.

'Good day sir,' he said, adjusting his spectacles. 'I've been expecting you.'

I stared back at the man in surprise.

'Sorry,' I said. 'You must be mistaking me for someone else. You didn't know I was coming!'

'Oh, I knew, Mr Calvey,' he said. 'It is written.'

He took out a magnificent fob watch and checked the hour against the shop's clock, ticking on the far wall.

'Now, if you'd care to take a seat, we'll get down to business. Time is money, sir…time is money.'

I all but fell onto the chair. This day was getting odder by the minute, and I was fairly certain by now that I had sustained a concussion in my fall earlier, but apart from the throbbing from the lump, my head was suddenly clear. I felt fine but for the prickly sensation of being watched. I turned my head towards a heavy green curtain that was ever so slightly agape and there, by the light of an oil lamp, sat a wizened old woman at a loom. I smiled, uncomfortable at being observed, but she never returned my smile, merely sat motionless, watching me with rheumy eyes.

'Here we are, sir,' the weaver said. I turned to him for a second and then turned back to the curtain. The old woman had gone! As silently as if she hadn't moved at all. My head suddenly became cloudy and I shook the fuzziness from it. The room spun slightly but then it cleared.

'Sir?' said the old man. 'Your fabric, sir.'

I didn't bother asking how he knew I was there to buy cloth. I just supposed a good percentage of his customers were. I looked down at the proffered roll of fabric resting on his outstretched arms and gave a small cry of surprise. It was the most beautiful thing I had ever seen and looked to have been expertly hand-woven with fine skeins of pure gold. It was breathtakingly beautiful, so delicate and fine it was, but as I looked at it, it seemed to change not only in texture, but in colour too, now the palest blue, now deep red…

I looked with amazement at the weaver, who wore a curious smile, and followed his eyes back down to the offering. I could hardly believe what I saw. The fabric was now patterned like rolling clouds! I did a double-take when I realised it actually was *made* of rolling clouds, wispy and fine and so soft, and it was moving, undulating. Waves of fabric tumbling along, as if toyed with by a gentle summer breeze. The weaver placed it in my arms, and I was amazed by how light and soft it was. It felt just like air.

'What is it? I cried in awe. 'It's exquisite.'

'Why sir, it's the very fabric of time,' said the weaver, with a wry smile. I looked at him, my brow furrowed.

'I can't possibly afford something like this,' I said, reluctant to hand it back.

'But sir, you must take it. It was woven especially for you!'

Suddenly my vision swam before me. I dropped the material and grabbed the arms of the chair as the room began to spin. I felt violently sick, and every so often the weaver's smiling face came into view, only his smile had changed, become somehow sinister. I heard his word's over and over. 'Why sir, it's the very fabric of time… the very fabric of time…' and then all went black.

I came round in the street, in a shop doorway, and looked up into the ruddy, jovial face of a man. There were boxes strewn at my feet…

'Ye all right pal?' he asked me as my eyes flickered open.' I didnae see ye there, ken? Over ma messages!'

Part Two

Summer

The train doesn't stop here anymore.

Its metal trail still weaves its way through the hollow, like an enormous asp, its huge rusting carcass shimmering in the heat. The tiny, archaic station with its handsome Victorian waiting room, refreshment room and ticket office stands frozen in time, like a still from *Brief Encounter*.

The tables in the refreshment room are abundant with dust. The old moon-faced clock in the waiting room still keeps time with rigorous precision, as though ghostly fingers tirelessly wind it night after night…after night.

It is summer in the valley. The crag is alive with wild flowers, bluebells and daffodils,
and untamed, the vibrant, scarlet rosebuds.

Standing aloft its highest point, the old school playing-field observes the river, winding its way idly through the lush green, only to lose itself deep below the lofty rock-carved incline and the vast, gaping mouth of the tunnel.

But the train doesn't stop here anymore.

Down in Lady's Valley, the baking rocks surpass the dim cool interior of its caves, and the leafy shade of the cinder path with its icy cold spring gives welcome retreat from the scorching heat. Come dusk, young lovers will cherish its aloofness, though some souls will beat a nervous retreat for fear of meeting the ghost of the long-extinct miner as he makes his way, laden with pick axe and lantern, toward the now-humbled pit head…

A wheel marks the spot where hundreds lost their lives.

It is summertime. The gaunt sashes of the old, old school cast light on dusty wooden desks and blackboards obscured in the silent, unoccupied classrooms.
Summertime in the village high street, the bustling shops, the market place.
It is summer in the park, the castle, the river, the crag.
The ancient church and the public house.
Yes it is summer in the valley where time stands still.

But the train doesn't stop here anymore …

The Critical Hour of 3a.m.

In the dawn, dim casting
I pace…
I pace.

I belong to no dimension.
Time neither enemy nor friend.
Darkness is the curse that halts all
progress,
but a darkness from within,
unaffected by sunlight.

For I am autumn,
even as I sit amongst the first
blooms of spring.
My skin like gossamer,
stretched tight over old bones, brittle
as chalk.

My nights, irrespective of time
seep into daylight hours
and the dawn steals silent past my
darkened window,
as if afraid to awaken the dead.

Still, in the silence of the night, I
hear her…
fleet of foot,

mute as a stone,
clearing away the cobwebs with her
cloth of silk.

While downstairs, in my shadowy
hallway,
the clock chimes the hour.

Of Neurosis

The world is too big.
I seek… confinement.
Sometimes!
In the middle of
An open field
I scream.

The world is too big.
The rabbit and
Mole know it, and
Burrow deep,
Deep into the
Unaffected sanctum
Of their lairs

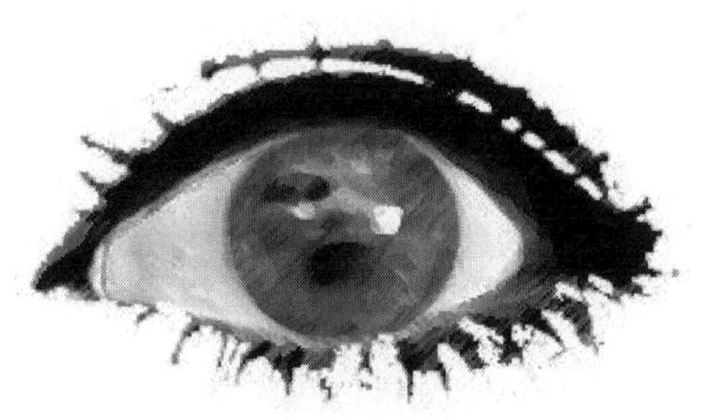

A London Particular or Thoughts upon Returning To a City I Loved (And Seeing Its Decline)

The night glistens wet, the pavement still
slippery from recent falls, and overhead
the incessant drip, drip, drip from bough to earth
and roof to gutter.

Tonight I walk alone. The darkness extends its
black, velvet-gloved hand and welcomes me
like a friend as I pass through its dismal streets
and alleys. There, fast food bins spill their
squally load onto the ground beneath, where rats
as big as cats skulk and feast amongst the
remains.

Still further along this hellish track, bare-footed
down-and-outs huddle together in groups for
warmth, their legacy combined in a brown felt
hat at their feet. Three shiny coins that glimmer,
sodden in the moonlight.

Deep into the heart of the city I go, past
theatres where yellowing fly posters proclaim
long-finished productions of Shakespeare and
Oscar Wilde. Past boarded-up shop windows
and green-painted brick walls declaring
provisions and senior service cigarettes. Past
public houses, long since rung their last orders.

Around me the city rots. Around me its inhabitants sleep. They dream tonight of its decline and their dreams are troubled…

Come tomorrow they'll wear their lines of burden with indifference, upon masks of everyday greet-the-world faces, which they remove every night and place for safekeeping into the antique hatboxes that hide in the dusty, shadowy depths beneath every bed.

But I look up tonight at their darkened windows, misted over with a thousand nocturnal sighs, and I can't help but wonder…

Do they even see this anymore?

Madam Rocha's Pastime

Act 1

Scene 1

We are in Francesca's apartment. It is early evening. We are in the dining room which is ready for a dinner party. To the left of the stage is a door which leads off to the kitchen, next to it a chaise. At the back is a door leading off to the hallway and the rest of the apartment. A large central table is set with full dinner service for four people and two large decanters of wine. On the back wall is a large ornate sideboard which opens to reveal bottles of spirits and glasses and an ice bucket and tongs. On top of the sideboard is a phone, a lamp and a glass half full of whiskey. To the right of the room is a large fireplace with the fire lit, and above a huge over-mantle with mirror. The mantle has a large clock, and a chandelier hangs central to the room.

FRANCESCA *sweeps in from the kitchen. She floats gracefully around the table making last minute adjustments so everything is perfect, before moving over to the mirror.*

Francesca …and of course I said to the caterers, you needn't wait on, not for four people…but darling how ludicrous! *(Pauses, takes a lipstick from her pocket and begins to apply it in the mirror)* I'm sure I'm more than capable of attending to three guests (*laughs*)…and then there's the wine. Of course, darling you don't know, do you? Well, what a debacle that was. Darling, Harvey Nicks promised me faithfully to deliver a case of Châteaux Neuf, '93 vintage, of course. I requested it be added to my weekly delivery, meaning I should have had them yesterday*…(plumps up her hair in the mirror*) at the very latest…

JAMES *her fiancé calls to her from the bedroom*

James (*off stage)* Franc, have you seen my blue shirt? The one with the…

Francesca In the closet darling, next to the Prince of Wales check trousers. I picked it up from the dry cleaners Thursday…and do hurry, they'll be here soon and you know how I dislike answering the front door…anyhow when my delivery came, guess what? No Chateaux Neuf…my dear I was quite beside myself. I phoned the store and the manager told me the shipment was late coming from France, and they hoped to have it Tuesday at the latest, darling… *(puts her hand on her chest*) roast leg of lamb, and no Neuf, can you imagine such a thing?

JAMES *comes into the room, looking bedraggled. He grins mischievously.* FRANCESCA *offers her cheek and he kisses it.*

James It hardly bears thinking about.

FRANCESCA *straightens his collar, turns him around, adjusts his jacket and begins picking off bits of fluff and brushing it down with her fingers*

Francesca Really James, you're the only man I know who can wear Armani and still manage to resemble a street urchin. *(sighs)* And do you think we might lay off the sarcasm *(pause)* for one night? It really is quite unbecoming…

JAMES *pulls away and goes over to the sideboard. He mixes FRANCESCA a drink and then takes his own from off the top. JAMES walks over to FRANCESCA with the drink.*

Francesca Luckily I found a bottle or two of something unpleasant from Oddbins hanging around. You know those bottles we purchased should your friends pay a visit. *(She sits on the chaise)* It should suffice for Cara, poor girl. Really she's quite without an education and I feel sure she knows not her Pinot Noir from her Shiraz. *(Pause)* I naturally will take au mineral.

James *(Still smiling)* Naturally. (*He drinks then takes his empty glass over to the sideboard)* What time are they due to arrive?

The doorbell rings. FRANCESCA *jumps up*

Francesca Oh dear, they're quite early… such ill breeding. (*pause)* Really, etiquette forbids such poor time-keeping

FRANCESCA *hurries into the kitchen and* JAMES *goes through the back door. We hear the ticking of the clock. Offstage we hear the door open and the muffled salutations. On set the chandelier dims, flickers and begins to sway. In the Kitchen* FRANCESCA *begins to sing loudly and tunelessly. We see shadows dance around the set walls. The door is opened at the back and* JAMES, ARMAND *and* CARA *enter.*

James FRANCESCA, OUR GUESTS HAVE ARRIVED… (*Lowers his voice and winks at Cara)* Probably having a go at the cooking sherry… *(Walks to the sideboard)* Drink anyone?

Francesca *(from the kitchen)* I'll be out in a minute darling. I'm just finishing off the mint sauce.

JAMES *fills his glass and turns to the couple.* CARA *and* ARMAND *look uncomfortable. They know about the caterers.*

James Ahem… (*Holds aloft his glass,)* Armand old boy?

Armand I'll join you in a scotch, thanks.

James Water, ice?

Armand No, I'll take it straight, thanks. (*He blushes when he realises what he's said)*

James *(He raises an eyebrow and smiles at Armand)* Mmm, what a waste… *(Sighs)* Cara?

Cara Not for me, thanks.

JAMES and ARMAND *stand talking at the sideboard.* CARA *wanders over to the fireplace and stands looking into the fire.* FRANCESCA *breezes in from the kitchen and all three stand to attention.*

Francesca Darlings…

She walks over to ARMAND *arms open and grabs his hands before offering her cheek.* ARMAND *kisses* FRANCESCA. *She turns and does the same to* CARA

Francesca Cara…mwah, mwah (*she kisses the air to either side of Cara's face)* Why my dear, you look lovely as usual…really such a pretty dress, you quite put me to shame…Truly it's amazing how you always manage to look so nice (*pause)* and on so… limited a budget… (*Turning to* JAMES*)* James, Cara hasn't got a drink…really darling, must I do everything?

FRANCESCA *leads* CARA *to the table and sits her down*

Cara Really, no I'm …

Francesca Nonsense, do try this new Australian Chardonnay, it's to die for…really for provincials they are becoming quite adept at wine making, but of course they have the climate out there, don't they? (*turning to* JAMES, *sharply)* Darling, the first course…

Scene 2

The lights dim and the action freezes, all we hear is the clock. Time is suspended for fifteen seconds when the lights return all four are seated at the table, half way through the meal. We return to laughter from around the table.

Francesca Really James, you're priceless… *(Has her hand on* JAMES*' arm, squeezes affectionately and lets go*) but truly, I believe, all one can hope for in life is to be happy.

James But surely Francesca, the human condition cannot allow for such a thing.

Armand All happiness is an illusion. We all need something to strive for and the pursuit of happiness can, in itself, bring about a kind of contentment *(pause)* a temporary reprieve as it were from one's pain…

FRANCESCA *picks up her napkin, folds it and lays it down again.* FRANCESCA *fingers the stem of her glass*

Francesca *(smirking)* Why Armand, surely you have found happiness in your relationship in Cara? Would you have us believe that this situation in which you find yourself is one of grief and suffering? *(She turns to* ARMAND*)*

Armand I…I mean only that mere existence itself brings about… *(He reaches over and takes Cara's hand.* CARA *stares at him coldly and doesn't respond*) But of course I love Cara dearly…

FRANCESCA, *still smiling, drinks from her glass.* JAMES *is fingering the rim of his glass.* JAMES *also sits back with a sneer; it is aimed at Armand.* ARMAND *feels uncomfortable and shifts awkwardly on his chair.*

Francesca *(laughing)* Darling, I tease. *(winks at James)* Really anyone can see you are the most devoted couple…

FRANCESCA *stands and looks at Cara.* CARA *glares at Francesca.* FRANCESCA *taps lightly twice on the side of her nose. We have silence for fifteen seconds. The characters freeze. The clock again becomes audible and the lights flicker.*

Francesca Cara darling, I'm thinking of doing something with my hair. It really is quite dreadful. I was hoping you could advise me yours always looks so… natural.

Cara Really Francesca, I doubt there is anything I could teach you *(pause)* and anyway you know you have beautiful hair. You're always being told so.

Francesca Then perhaps you will help me with dessert…we can leave the gentlemen to their *(gives a sly look to James)* …small talk.

FRANCESCA *and* CARA *leave though the kitchen door, taking plates and cutlery with them.* JAMES *takes a cigarette from his pocket.*

Francesca *(from the kitchen)* Kindly refrain from smoking at the dinner table, James.

JAMES *grins at* ARMAND *and lights the cigarette.*

ARMAND So James, soon to be wed, are you ready to give up your debauched lifestyle and settle down in domestic bliss?

James *(laughing)* Darling, I'll never give up debauchery. It's my only vice.

JAMES *leans over to Armand and strokes his arm flirtingly.* ARMAND *is uncomfortable.* JAMES *takes hold of Armand's hand and moves in so their faces are close.*

James But perhaps I can persuade you to join me at my club…

Scene 3

FRANCESCA'S bedroom, a couple of hours later. There is a large bed in the centre of the room, two bedside cabinets with lamps. The one on the left also has a book on it. To the far right-hand side of the bed is the door. JAMES *is in bed reading.* FRANCESCA *is applying face cream at her dressing table which is at the foot of the bed.*

Francesca ...but of course you realise, Armand is hopelessly in love with me…

James (*without looking up)* Really? I had thought I was the object of his affections.

Francesca How can you be so silly, darling? Armand isn't homosexual.

James *(Licks his finger and turns the page)* Does Cara know that?

FRANCESCA *joins* JAMES *in bed.*

Francesca Really, Cara is a silly creature and quite unworthy of Armand. Neither his social nor intellectual equal. He should find himself an educated lady with good connections. He really is rather handsome don't you agree?

James *(looks up from his book and grins)* Well, I wouldn't banish him from my boudoir for breaking…

Francesca *(Shocked)* James, how can you be so vulgar? Really I…

James *(laughing)* But perhaps *you* should bring a little colour back into his otherwise dull existence.

JAMES *puts down his book, yawns, stretches and lays back on his pillow.* FRANCESCA *turns to him sharply.*

Francesca James, how preposterous…what an extraordinarily inappropriate suggestion. I…I'm quite lost for words.

FRANCESCA *fluffs up her pillows and turns to James who is resting his eyes***.** FRANCESCA *smiles.*

Francesca Truly darling I'm appalled, asking such a thing of a lady…your own fiancée at that…I despair of you. Really James, I sometimes wonder at your upbringing. *(pause)* Naturally I would never dream of doing so abhorrent a thing (*pauses and flattens out her bedding with her palms)* …Of course my love, there's nothing stopping you from suggesting to Armand that there are in fact other options open to him than to settle for a young lady quite unworthy of his affections…Of course I am truly fond of Cara, but I am equally convinced that she would be happier with a gentleman more disposed to her own social standing and circumstances. *(Pause)* Yes I know it's immoral, but really it would be to their mutual benefit…James. (*louder)* James.

James *(half asleep)* Uh-huh.

Francesca (*settles back on her pillow with a smile)* Then you'll do it darling, for the sake of one's poor unfortunate friends?

James Uh.

FRANCESCA *picks up her own book from her bedside cabinet, reads a line and then puts it down*

Francesca Perhaps darling, you might introduce him to one of your friends, one of those intellectuals from your book club, or a nice young lady…or gentleman *(pause)* from the university…

FRANCESCA *puts her book back on the table*

Francesca Perhaps, my love…you might seduce him?

FRANCESCA *turns to JAMES*

Francesca James… (*Louder)* James.

James *(snores in response)*

Francesca Well, really.

Lights fade.

Part Three

Autumn

Who's to care if migrating hoards flee south, robbing the dawn of birdsong and leaving the sky laden but devoid of flight save for the jet? That metal crow, slicing through autumnal cloud and leaving in its wake a vapour trail, slow in its disbursement in the thick, treacle atmosphere.

A heart can be at peace with this season. When nature wears a mask more beautiful than that she chooses to greet the seasons past and seasons yet to come.

So we wade ankle deep, with spirits that soar, through the rich golden carpet lining our parks and avenues, and observe the scattered misanthropist who, with cheeks pinched and collar turned, dots this flaxen landscape.
Still, autumn for all her splendour is a cruel mistress, and we feel with every blast of wind and jolt of bone the arthritic movement of an aged and dying year.

Nothing stirs beneath the pond's glacial façade, and leaves, tokens of the bowing gods, float upon its motionless surface like dead babies. The trees are not embarrassed by their nakedness, in contrast with the bush, as heavy with plot as labour. Relieved of her load by the last of this day's pickers, who gather in abundance. Whilst somewhere, far, far away in his field, the farmer rapes the acre.

Light is fading as a watery sun sinks into an ever-darkening landscape, turning the city from golden, to orange, to red, the trees omnipotent against the evening sky. The branches of a twisted oak tap eerily against the park railings, and rooting in the undergrowth, some manner of beast flees to the safety of its dark confine.
Overhead, chimneys begin to smoke.
Autumn's at her palate and the world is crimson.
And above heads, shrouded in tree hollows, the squirrels hoard.

Last Night I Dreamed of Joseph

In my hunger, I shall devour you.
So timeless glides each booted foot and
Silken slipper across the parched, marble floor.
Graceful. Ever graceful, dancers as far as the
eye can see.

Still, beyond.
Far beyond the star-lit patio, where
Lovers woo beneath watchful eye of a
White moon mother.
Beyond the glade where fairies dwell,
Parodies of long forgotten childhood dreams.

Beyond the old stone where the water runs
black.
There, something unmentionable stirs.
Beyond that yet, far, far beyond the green-
tipped wood,
Where naked pygmies squeal and chase.
Squeal…

And chase.
There, just above the silent,
Calm surface of purest, white light, untouched
yet
Sits you, my beautiful Narcissus.
Cupid's dream. Incarnate of the gods…

Spellbound by those eyes of flaming amber.
Keeper of hearts. Destiny's child. A wandering
spirit, unblemished by life.

Yet, deep below in the silent water, sits,
Watching, waiting…Contemplating, a life in all
its entirety

The echo of my godself.

Albert

The mist crept down the silent, empty street, seeking out and filling every nook and crevice with its probing, ghostly fingers. The sky was a patchwork of amber and grey as dawn broke through, reducing the darkness to mere shadows that retreated into the deepest corners, there to hide like guilty secrets until the following sunset. The streetlamp's dismal glow was lost to the ether and neighbouring cats, those nocturnal prowlers, slunk off home in search of breakfast and a cosy lap.

Sam stared at the dying embers of his hearth, his eye falling on the clock on the mantle. Five thirty-five. Over seven hours had passed since his act of heroism or stupidity, or both, had led him to firstly rescue a homeless man from four savages intent on doing him harm, and then secondly, to offer said old man a bed for the night. The same old man who now lay dead in his spare room, still clutching the old suitcase he'd fought so bravely to keep.

Sam was thirty and lived alone. Through choice, that is, and not the lack of it. He worked as a freelance photographer, and being an artist, people interested him. That's how he'd come to know Old Albert, the man who lay cooling in his spare room. Often seen around King's Cross station, Albert was friendly and popular with regular travellers, shopkeepers and railway workers and could often be seen chatting with the station staff and passengers. Never once did he ask anyone for money, although his clothes were rags and he clearly lived rough. This and the fact that he was never seen without an old suitcase, to which he clung desperately, led people to think Albert was an eccentric millionaire and that his precious suitcase probably contained the family jewels. Albert would merely smile and hold it tightly against his chest, giving nothing away.

Sam thought Albert would make a brilliant subject for a new photography project and offered to pay him to model, but Albert had refused all offers of money and said he'd be happy to help. In a cut-throat world based on profit and gain, Sam thought him a gentleman indeed, one of a dying breed. In finding time to chat with him, Sam was surprised to learn that Albert was not only worldly and interesting, but well-spoken and frighteningly intelligent too.

Sam lit a cigarette, holding tightly onto the match until it burned away to a blackened stump in his charred fingers. It felt good, the pain. It felt real! He inhaled deeply.

What was he to do? Should he go to the police? It would surely look dodgy, him taking the old man in for the night, what with the rumours about the contents of the case. That bloody case, the mysterious suitcase that Albert fought so hard to keep. What was in it that Albert should protect it with his life?

For what seemed like the millionth time that night, Sam paced the floor, nervously chewing at his nails. What if he had died of his injuries?

Oh God, Sam thought. *I should have called an ambulance, took him to hospital*. But Albert had refused to go, wanting only a hot bath, a brandy and a warm bed.

"Oh shit!" Sam groaned. "Shit, shit, shit!"

He sunk to his knees and bowed his head, his weary eyes making monsters of the swirling shapes in the carpet.

A sudden feeling of remorse and sadness overcame him. A man had died, someone he knew, someone he liked, and died in a most horrible way. Reluctantly, he got up and made his way across the hall to his spare room-come studio.

He was dead alright, the old man, Albert. His sightless eyes stared at the ceiling, not shiny like the eyes of a dead fish, but masked by a film. Dead, dull eyes. Sam tried to close them but he couldn't, and he flinched at the feel of Albert's rapidly cooling waxen skin. He was about to cover the old man with a sheet when he noticed the case was missing. Sam's heart skipped a beat and his eyes searched the room furiously. Where could it be, that damn suitcase?

Sam threw back the sheets to cover Albert's face. His unkempt white hair, clean after his bath, had fallen about him on the pillow. His world-weary face, swollen in places from the beating he received, read like a map of the underground. Lines, etched into his skin, beating a path from the corners of his eyes and mouth, seemed to converge around the soft, fleshy mounds of his cheek. He must have been a handsome man once, Sam mused and again felt an enormous feeling of sadness and pity come over him.

In pulling up the sheets, Sam had uncovered the old man's feet and there, with Albert's legs resting on it, was the suitcase. Sam held his breath as he carefully removed it, sheepishly glancing at Albert's head as he did so, half expecting him even in death to rise up in anger and defend his treasured possession. Albert of course remained as still and silent as the grave. Sam covered him and left the room.

Sam had been to Berkshire to photograph a society wedding. It was boring work, but it paid well. He had missed the last direct train to London Victoria, resulting in him not returning to King's Cross until nearly midnight. He was tired and badly needed a drink. Suddenly, he heard a cry. A gang of youths had someone cornered in a shop doorway and were kicking and hurling abuse at the poor defenceless creature.

Sam, not the most physical of men, had charged towards the lads shouting to his lungs' full capacity, rage and fear spurring him on, adrenalin fuelling his launch. The lads had panicked and run away, much to Sam's relief. He had no doubt in his mind that they could have done him real damage had they chosen to do so. He noticed the case first, clutched tightly in the arms of this poor bloodied creature, one arm still shielding his face.

"Albert?" he cried. "Albert, it's me Sam. Are you ok? Can I get you an ambulance?"

Sam grimaced when he saw the damage the thugs had done. One of Albert's eyes was almost entirely closed and was already beginning to swell. His nose looked broken, and blood and spittle foamed at the corners of his mouth. Sam felt his heart pounding in his chest, bile rising in his throat.

"S-Sam?" the old man managed to say. His breath came in short, rasping succession, and Sam suspected a broken rib or two.

"Albert, I need to get you to hospital."

"No, no!" Albert hissed waving his arm in a dismissive gesture. "No police or hospitals. Just please, help me up, Sam."

Sam carefully took Albert by the arm, supporting him to minimise the old man's pain. Still Albert winced with every move.

"Albert, if you won't see a doctor, please come home with me, just for tonight."

Sam had sat Albert down and poured him a large brandy before allowing himself the same. Albert's breathing was laboured and shallow. He rested his chin on his chest, clearly worn out, and spoke very little. Sam offered to run a bath and Albert readily accepted. After a good hour soaking, Albert had emerged in Sam's old jogging suit, looking better.

Sam tried to engage him in conversation to assess his condition, but Albert was exhausted and wanted only to rest, so Sam led him to his studio which doubled up as a spare bedroom. That was the last time he'd seen the old man alive. Tiredness weighed heavy on him, but Sam had found himself unable to sleep. Around three in the morning he'd dropped in to check on the old man, only to find him lifeless on the bed.

Sam now sat looking at the suitcase, eyeing it cautiously, reservedly, as though it might at any time spring open and by sheer will alone reveal its contents to him. Should he open it? Would he be in trouble for doing so? Who would know?

Albert would, his conscience pricked him.

Sam shook his head, vainly trying to shake off the tiredness and the voices that whispered, one in each ear, human nature tempting him to open the case, propriety entreating him not to.

He absentmindedly fingered the clasp. It was one of the old style cases, hard leather with clasps instead of a zip. It had certainly seen better days and was covered in scuffs and scratches.

He must open the case, he had decided. If only for some clue to Albert's identity. His fingers trembled as he tried the clasp.

This is ridiculous, Sam told himself.

A steely resolve and sheer determination suddenly kicked in and he flipped the clasp with both hands. Nothing happened. Sam held his breath and the world was still. From somewhere in the distance, a car alarm sounded and the birds responded with a dawn chorus. The sparrow, the jay, then the blackbird.

They're telling my secret, thought Sam. Frustration overcame him as he fumbled with the clasp.

Open, open, he silently willed it, but the case wouldn't budge. It was locked. He needed the key.

"Damn it!" he yelled. "Where is the bloody key?"

Albert's clothes lay in a crumpled heap in the corner and although they were shabby and old, they were surprisingly clean and fresh. Sam searched in every pocket and found nothing but holes and bits of fluff. He even checked Albert's boots and socks. Nothing!

“Nnnnoooooooo!” Sam moaned. The need to open the case and see what the man had thought worth dying for had intensified with every minute that passed. He ran over to where the case lay and again tried the clasp, and again…and again.

“Aaaaarrrggghhhhhhhhh!” he cried. Tears of rage and frustration ran in rivulets down his burning cheeks. He lifted the case above his head, shook it viciously and then threw it against the wall. It hit hard, bounced off and came to rest at his feet. Sam stared wide-eyed at the case as though it were suddenly a thing of menace. Then he heard a click. He saw the clasp turn and all at once, as though finally succumbing, yielding to his will, the case sprung open.

Sam held his breath and again the world grew silent. Only the monotonous ticking of his mantle clock, matching stroke by stroke the hammering of his heart, was audible. The blood coursing through his veins seemed deafeningly loud in his ears, and beads of perspiration decorated his brow like thousands of tiny crystals. He dropped to his knees on the floor.

Inside the case were photographs, and letters yellow with age, all written by the same hand and tied neatly in a bow. Sam put the letters, all signed 'Forever yours, my darling…May xxx,' to one side while he studied the photographs. One was a wedding photo, a handsome young soldier bearing an uncanny resemblance to Albert, and a beautiful young bride, her eyes shining with happiness and an expectation that could not be dulled by the deterioration of a photograph or by the passing of time. There were later photographs too, of the young couple and two boys, family portraits capturing a memory, stills immortalised, frozen in time, as only a photograph could be.

There were also legal documents, birth and death certificates, Albert having long outlived the rest of his family, a de-mob certificate, an old passport, and official war documents. Albert it seemed, or Corporal Charles Albert Taylor-Fitch of the 3rd Battalion, Royal Artillery Gun Corps to give him his full title, was not only well-decorated, but was awarded with the VC for acts of extreme bravery, above and beyond his call of duty in battle. Sam searched for any medals, but they were probably long gone, presumably pawned by Albert in order to buy food or clothing.

Sam sat back against the sofa, suddenly overcome by a deep feeling of loss. So the thing Albert had given his life to protect from thieves *was* his life. His life in pictures, in documents, in the written word. All of his memories together in one suitcase, a cargo more precious by far than any money or jewels.

Sam thought of the old man lying dead in his back room. Of the kind, worldly gentleman, the decorated war hero, reduced to living on the streets like a stray dog, his whole life packed up, consigned to a battered old suitcase.

From outside on the Pentonville Road came sounds of life, a dustcart passing and a man shouting. From nearby, a dog barked, then howled piteously. The sound came thin and hollow in the crisp morning air. London was awake. A new day had begun. Soon the sounds of buses and taxis outside would be deafeningly loud, a sound that barely even registered anymore.

Sam, curled tightly in a foetal ball on the floor of his lounge, buried his face in his hands and wept.

Inspired

(An Ode to Marshall Mathers)

Your words got me stirring; they've got my
brain whirring,
Like some kind of maelstrom. A twister on the
horizon.
Full speed like a stallion. I float like a galleon.
I'm
Marching headlong to the fight, like battalions
Of soldiers who know that they're going to die,
Never to see how their mothers will cry.
But still these words tumble and spill in my
brain
Like balls in a dryer, and I'm going insane
With their tippity-tappity-tippity-tap. And even
at
Night when I'm taking a nap, your words they
surround me
Like a murder in flight, and haunt all my dreams
like a ghost
In the night.

Your lyric has passion, your words found a
voice.
As a poet you inspire me. As a performer you
tire me.
Your energy boundless, your example has found
us,

Even at night when the shadows surround us,
Red-eyed at our desks, as we struggle for words,
Even as they fly round our heads just like birds.
Waiting to be plucked from the air like a kite,
caught
On the wind and soaring at heights. But
prisoners really
Attached to a string, never quite free like the
crow on the wing.
Just waiting to be brought down to earth in a
rage and forever
Made captive, just words on a page.

Just A Thought

Getting older is taking stock. No longer sweating the small stuff. Accepting the que sera and the peace this brings. The calmness is exquisite, like an acceptance of death without actually dying. It is an acceptance of oneness, of the can do's and the unobtainable and being resigned to what is unattainable. Not losing your purpose but the realisation of your true purpose. Not letting go of all your dreams, but focusing on what can actually be realised. With this development also comes an acceptance of the self and a nearing to wholeness.

Part Four

Winter

No zephyr this that rants and raves, moans and
howls, screaming demented through the eves.
The shops bedecked with holly wreath and
festive trimming know not of my gloom.

Winter has come to town, a winter iron-hard and
bitter.
No beauty this ice queen virgin, her kiss of
death still fresh as morning dew on cheek of
blue-lipped hypothermic.

Still, children, robin's breast red-cheeked and
shiny-eyed, hang stockings on mantles,
expectant.

From the four corners of gay Paris,
townswomen bustle and screech, whilst fat-
fingered spouses roll Napoleon's wage in
crystal-cut goldfish-bowl glasses.
Outside, the causeway glistens white and the
snowflakes swirl and dance to the wind's tune.

Few individuals brave the blizzards tonight.
The spirit's flame dances in my throat, while
shadows finish their nightly jaunt and glide into
obscurity beneath skirting and behind doors.

To bed, my ghosts ever present by my side.
Goodnight remorse, regret, loneliness,
bitterness, anger.
Put yourselves to bed and don't forget to turn
out the light.
The fire is dying as the wind races down the
chimney and red-hot embers leap to their final
resting place on the hearth.

Outside, the cruel hand of winter tears slates
from the roof, and invisible fingers rattle at the
casement.
The snowflakes are playing chase. The moon
stands frozen in her halo, and the wind howls
like a banshee.

Somewhere, a distant bell peals as shadows
fade to grey, and dawn begins, with ghostly
vines, to filter through a laden sky.

A Christmas Ghost

Everything had stopped; it was almost like waiting to breathe. Sound seemed far away and it wasn't cold anymore. My feet had been freezing all day. I only had my sneakers on. The soles were thin and one of them had a hole. My Mam had plugged it with cardboard to keep the rain out, but it just made the cardboard soggy. I was ok because I was wearing my snorkel. It had been my brother's and was two sizes too big, but at least it was warm.

I should have been at school really, not in town, but I wanted to see the Christmas shops. Everywhere was busy. The windows were full of toys and Johnson's had a real train set in it, a steam loco all set up, tunnel and all. Lewis' had a dinosaur, big as me, that roared and moved its head. All the shops had sparkling lights and trees as tall as houses.

When I got really cold, I stood by the fire where a man was roasting chestnuts. The smell made me so hungry my belly rumbled, and the man gave me a nut. It was so hot that I dropped it in the snow. He laughed at me.

I tried to sneak into Debenhams to see Father Christmas. Security man said I was a ruffian and should be at school. I argued that I was poorly and anyhow Father Christmas would see me, ruffian or not. I got a clip around the ear for my cheek.

I was set to try the other door when I saw him. The man on the railway bridge. The bridge was very old and stood high above the road. It was odd, because there was no footpath up there, only the railway line. He looked funny too, sort of dark and wearing old-fashioned clothes. I tried to make out his face. I couldn't see one, just blackness, and what was strange was, now, I couldn't move. I tried to turn away but my legs wouldn't work. I couldn't close my eyes, couldn't stop staring at the strange man on the bridge, and then he jumped.

That's when the world stood still, it seemed like forever, then suddenly I could move my head. I looked up, the sky was full of snow and it was falling on my face. I tried to scream, but no sound came out. Then slowly, like in a dream, time came back. The noise of the traffic, the busy street, the smell of chestnut and wood smoke and the bitter cold that went right through me. Then I did scream.

'Are you all right, son?'

The old man was shaking me. His face was close and I could smell beer and oldness on him.

'The man, is he…' I couldn't speak for a moment. 'Is he dead?' I finally stammered. 'The man on the bridge.'

He looked at me like I was daft. I looked over the road. There was no one there! By now there was a crowd around me. A woman from Debenhams pushed through.

'Bring the lad inside,' she said.

I looked up at her painted face and silly hair. She looked kind and I gave her my best little-boy-lost smile.

'You think I'd be able to see Father Christmas?' I said.

Nocturne

Above,
The inky, speckled sky
And all is stilled by gentle hush.

So pure the
Dreams of sleeping babes.
And sweet, each mother's lullaby.

But from each
Dark, secluded place,
Nocturnal creatures start to roam.

As each door
Closes on the night.
So every eye concludes the form

Of shadows who
Merge to cease the light.
And every class of bashful

Shade, begins
To dance with grace, so vague and
Leave the corners, where they fade,

As each
New dawn brings sun's sweet

Kiss, an angel chorus greets the day.

But now each
Dusky hour is theirs. Mischievous
With each game they play, on

Weary eye
And leaden head,
Inert on pillow, though mind's

Awake and
Prey to all these twilight
Wraiths and pray for oblivion to take their
place.

While those in slumber's troubled grip
Paralysed in rest each muscle twitch
Each woeful moan from parted lip

As the night, a sleeping viper,
Uncoils with a hiss

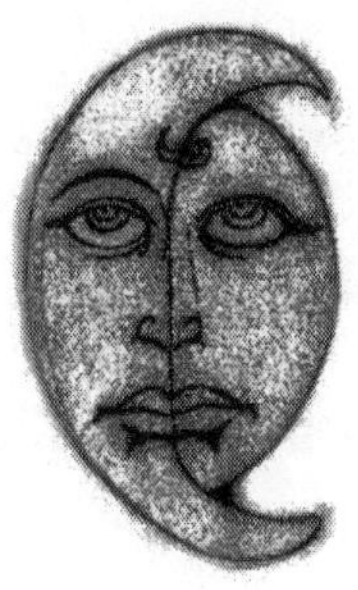

Alan

(From No.41 Burlington Road)

You're going to die, you tell your reflection. It's as if you're passing on the burden to someone else.

When you first learn of this, you are numbed. You feel nothing. You wait for the fear that's inevitably to come. Even so, when it hits, you're not prepared for the assault.

Fear like this sneaks up on you from below. You stand still too long, like a tree, and it creeps up around you. A parasitic thing, it clings to you for sustenance and you feed it. It invades you and once inside, it paralyses with an iron grip, like ice-cold fingers around your heart. Your lungs fight for air and your stomach knots like a ball of wool.

No-one or nothing can free a man from his fear. You're too entwined, too connected…you try to sleep, to escape…to forget.

In the morning, fear has etched its procession upon your face.

Pandora's Box

Around Vesta's marble hearth they sit,
Crimson-lipped and gossamer.
Their chastity a dagger, that
Thrusts its mortal wound deep
Into the sides
Of men, of sinners
Iron-limbed and noble
Nursing a hurt.
Equally blessed and cursed they roam
In packs, mindless.
Of no mind.
Their fate sealed.
Spawned of a rotten society.
A trail of destruction in their wake.
Fertile…
But no father figure.
The mighty titan slain for what?
Wars were fought and lost
And won…
Alone in his hotel room
One man fights a battle to the death
With his wallpaper.
He loses, but
His death does not go unmarked.
For in his wake
His passing has
Opened the box,

Unleashing upon
An unsuspecting world
The furies of those
Long gone…

Old Ma Barker's Sovereign

The cottage was a low, ivy-clad, stone-built house with small windows and a weathered picket fence, behind which the headless stems of rose bushes stirred gently in the breeze.

Inside, a rabbit warren of small rooms and winding corridors led to a farmhouse kitchen dominated by an old enamelled stove. A heavily laden pine dresser covered one wall. From racks on the wall hung pots, pans and jelly moulds of all shapes and sizes, and a glazed stable door lead out to a small but pretty garden.

In the lounge, dark oak beams cut across the low ceiling, and the well-worn floorboards were covered by a pretty pegged rug, giving the space an intimate, lived-in feeling. The soot-clad inglenook housed a well-used dog grate, to which clung embers of some long-dead fire, like a cherished memory. To one side of the grate, logs were piled high and a large black hook, presumably for a kettle, had been pushed back into the wall. The other side housed a tiny sequestered nook into which one could curl up tight on a cold winter's night and watch as the flames raced up the chimney.

A crooked dog-leg staircase wound its way upward, the top of which looked shadowy and mysterious. Upstairs however all was equally twee and homely. Two small bedrooms sat to the front of the house and a curious L-shaped room and a fair-sized bathroom, housing a huge iron bath on ball and claw feet, were at the rear.

It was to the strangely shaped bedroom I was drawn. It seemed to be built into the eves, for at one corner the roof pitched so low there was barely space to stand. The tiny window looked out into the garden and tucked in around the corner. Occupying its own private space was an old iron bedstead, dressed with a faded patchwork eiderdown. A small grate had been built into the chimney breast and a threadbare old rug obscured the dusty floorboards. Over by the window was a well-beaten, scratched-up wooden desk, and it was in the drawer of this desk that I found it.

As I gingerly opened the drawer, which given its age ran surprisingly smoothly, I was hit by a musty, cloying smell that seemed to stick to my hair and clothes before moving about the room as though led by a draught. It was almost as if in opening the drawer I had released a ghost, a memory, a fragment of the past, trapped there many years before.

The room seemed to shimmer before my eyes and I grabbed the desk, suddenly feeling light-headed, and then equally swiftly the sensation lifted. I looked into the drawer, but much to my disappointment found it was empty. I was about to shut it when a small voice in the back of my mind told me to look again. Apprehensively, I searched the dark recesses of the drawer, almost squealing when a spider ran across my hand, disturbed from its hiding place in some dark corner.

Eventually I found something that felt cold to the touch and groaned inwardly, thinking I'd risked death by spider, not to mention countless splinters, only to find a two-pence coin. I pulled my hand out and the coin with it and stared in awe. Although blackened with age and dirt, it was unmistakably a gold sovereign. I fingered it with disbelief, turning it around in the palm of my hand.

Suddenly the hair prickled on the back of my neck and the room turned icy cold. I slowly turned, my heart pounding, my mouth dry, and saw an old woman sitting on the edge of the bed, looking at me. I wanted to cry out but my throat felt restricted and I couldn't find the words. The old lady was as solid as you or I, but she seemed grey, as though her colours had faded with time. She never spoke, just smiled at me and held out her hand. I suddenly felt calm and peaceful and then, she was gone.

I wrapped my fingers around the coin and ran for stairs. Would I tell anyone about the coin, about the ghost of the kind old lady? I wondered. I smiled to myself. Somehow I knew that the coin was meant for me and this was to be our secret.

She

She is leaving!
Some watch her go
With a wistful sigh,
Others with a tear.
An air of sadness,
Like someone trying to capture
A memory, a thing
Of no substance.

I feel no remorse.
Like summertime she is bland.
Pretty, but with
Little character.
Nomadic, but no enigma.
All see her go
As are certain of her return.

On leaving, her replacement comes.
This I welcome like a log fire
When evenings draw in,
Sombre and menacing.
The sky laden, devoid of birds.
Though my heart is not yet
Moved to lament.

I favour this season.
Fresh and crisp,
She is chestnut and my flesh responds
To her kisses, breathless,
Singed beneath her scarlet lips.
Cold,
But no winter.

The Theatre Of Ghosts

A decadent stage set to perform.
Harpsichord, violins, clarinets.
The brightly-coloured costumes and
The painted-faced grotesques.

A gin-soaked crowd who cheered and sang.
Those brazen whores with scarlet lips.
A strident conductor and his band.
The tattered frock coats and the wigs.

A leading lady's swan song and
Those chorus girls with gartered thighs.
The cackling, Macbeth witches and
From Juliet, a love struck sigh.

The dried up, would-be thespian
Who played out every word,
With passion and with pathos,
Though he never trod these boards.

The jaded usher who walks the crowd.
To drunken jeers and to screams.
Priest, thief and hedonist meet tonight
In this theatre it seems.

From peeling gilded angels
To torn and filthy seats.
Now seedy, once magnificent
This theatre of dreams.

The careless lucifer that dropped
From loaded hand to back of seat.
The terror of a drunken crowd
Who struggled to their feet.

Such panic from performers, rapt
Upon the stage, like the frenzy
Of a wild beast, when
Trapped inside a cage.

The frailty of all who saw,
Mortality through that gin-soaked haze.
For death is cruel, it mirrors art
In any number of ways.

This burnt-out shell once more alive,
Though ghoulish are its hosts.
For each night show must, and does go on
In the theatre of ghosts.

Symphony in Red

A red smear like an angry mouth's
Emblazoned 'cross the noon late sky
And huddled in a crimson scarf
And woolen hat, a passer by
Gives life to Lazarus hands cupped tight,
With misted breath for all to see.
And autumn's offering, now old
Is laid to rest along the quay.
The streetlamp’s new lit scarlet glow
Upon the ether now is lost
And painted barges, red and gold
Are moored captive at their posts.

Auvers - But For The Grace Of God

(A memoir of France)

Auvers, the village of painters, was idyllic. It was situated on the river Oise, in the beautiful Val D'Oise, the garden of France, its winding lanes and small cottages making it every bit the chocolate-box village. The house itself was a beautiful cottage, set back off the beaten track with woodland to the rear.

It was a mild enough evening, and from the open window of the cottage came the smell of freshly-baked bread. As soon as I opened the gate, a big black dog came bounding out to meet me, barking joyously. I'd always had a dog so I could tell a friendly bark from a warning one, and I fell to my knees and cupped its head in my hands and rubbed its ears vigorously.

"Kellleeeeeeeee," called a voice from the somewhere around the side of the cottage "Kelly, regarde la balle!"

A plump, kindly-looking lady appeared by the side porch, waving a ball. The dog turned and bounded towards her, standing on its hind legs and pinning her to the wall in its effort to get the ball.

"Crazy dog, bad dog," she chided, never losing her smile.

"Ah, Monsieur Philleeps," she said, pushing the dog away and rushing over. "Very pleezed to meet you."

Inside, the cottage was as a cottage should be. There were plenty in our village, so although charming, it was nothing new. What was new, though, was the French-ness of it. In the kitchen was an huge enamelled stove from which emanated all manner of delicious smells, and the biggest dresser I had ever seen, which groaned under the weight of china and novelty tea pots, potted herbs and old framed photographs. From racks on the wall hung copper pans and moulds of all shapes and sizes, and from a wooden shelf above the cooker were strung dried herbs and flowers. A huge basket of fruit over-spilled onto a much-loved and much-scrubbed farmhouse table, at which I was promptly seated and served a huge earthenware pot of mouth-watering beef stew, with big chunks of warm French bread. While I was tucking in, she brought over a mug of creamy, fresh milk, the likes of which I'd never tasted before.

"Fresh from next door's farm," she told me proudly.

Later I was shown to a small room at the back of the house. As I sank into the soft mattress and covered myself up to the chin with the homemade eiderdown, I found myself bathed in a warm, fuzzy glow, a feeling completely alien to me, and I soon drifted off to sleep.

I was up bright and early next day, after the best night's sleep I had ever had. Soon after breakfast I heard a cheerful whistle, and a friendly face appeared at the kitchen window. It was apparently Betraud, our neighbour, with fresh eggs and milk from the farm.

"Ah, good morning, mon ami," he said to me in perfect English. "How did you sleep?"

I left no stone unturned in my exploration of Auvers. I was amazed to find it was the exact same village that Vincent had left, even down to the bunting outside the town hall. Vincent's café, or the Commerce de Vins restaurant as it is now called, was in the village's main street, with the Van Gogh museum upstairs. It consisted of two rooms, one of which was Vincent's bedroom and the room he died in and was directly opposite the town hall, straight from his painting, with the famous church up a small winding lane to the right and his grave in Le Cimetière, a good fifteen minutes' walk beyond the church, heading out of the village.

I had soon walked the walk, stopping off at a florist to buy sunflowers for Vincent's grave. At the graveside I was overcome by such a feeling of sadness and grief that I had to stand back against the wall to steady myself. I traced his name with my finger on the worn headstone. This was no grave for one so special. It was a humble, one would almost say poor grave, which of course Vincent was.

I was interrupted in my special moment by the arrival of three Japanese tourists, a man and two women armed with cameras, and I bid a resentful and hasty retreat. I watched them for a moment, feeling cheated. The man stepped on Vincent's grave and it seemed disrespectful to me. This was a peaceful place, a place for reflection, and I felt myself getting hot and a familiar red mist descending. I ran aimlessly, tears blinding, searing my already burning cheeks.

Back at the church I stopped, fighting to catch my breath, wondering again where these sudden uncontrollable rages came from. I knew I was behaving like a fool, that they had as much right to be there as me, but in my poor befuddled and immature mind he was my Vincent and only I shared and understood his pain. I can look back now and say quite calmly what an idiot I was, a typically arrogant youth.

I had walked back down the hill, feeling lonely, sad and homesick for a place and time that didn't exist, or no longer existed. I saw some live chicks in a patisserie window and thought it cruel and wanted to free them. I felt displaced as I had so many times before and ached for something I didn't yet know.

I bought some cheese, some bread and a half bottle of wine. I ate them by the Oise with the sun on my back and I suddenly felt at peace again. I lay with the sound of the river lapping gently at my feet, content in the long grass, and slept.

I was in love with the village and its people. Even so, I didn't see how I could stay. I had no money and I was due to go to Arts College that September. But I wanted to stay. Badly.

Soon Bertraud and I became good friends and it was he who got me a job on the farm helping to feed the animals and putting them to bed. The small wage and a top up sent by my dad, plus whatever I got for my paintings, were more than enough for me to live comfortably for the short time I was there. I had an arrangement with Madam Mathieu, or Marie-Juliette as I came to know her, whereupon I was to stay in her guest room when she had no bookings. Otherwise, I would sleep on the farm with Bertraud and Jean-Marc, another farm hand, which was an adventure for me, as it meant nights by the river, sipping wine in front of the campfire.

Bertraud and Jean-Marc were off to University in Paris that autumn and we had some really interesting conversations about art, literature and philosophy. Sometimes the conversation would get heated. When a couple of the other farm hands would join us, they were rough and uncultured and spoke no English, and I didn't like them very much. I always had the feeling they were ridiculing me, but Bertraud would step in and after much good-natured buffoonery and pretend fighting, they would dissolve into fits of raucous laughter and the good atmosphere would be restored.

So I spent my days painting and exploring the valley on Marie-Juliette's ancient bicycle, and my evenings working and drinking wine by the river with the boys. I worked hard on the farm and soon became strong and muscular and bronzed from my days spent outdoors.

I did quite well with my paintings, too, over the few months I was there. I seemed to develop my skills under what I felt was the watchful eye of my beloved Vincent and also with the help of a couple of local artists with whom I'd become friends. I was lucky enough to be part of a local exhibition at the Commerce de Vins, selling two paintings. My paintings were juvenile and crude compared to the real artists, but they were in the style of Vincent's and seemed popular enough with the tourists.

The summer passed by quickly and Betraud and Jean-Marc were getting ready to go to university. Although it was only thirty-five kilometres to Paris, they were staying on campus. Bertraud was from St. Denis originally and had come to the Valley to work over summer. I felt as though my stomach had been kicked in the day he left.

The evening before he went, he found me in Thomas' barn and gave me a silver St. Christopher, engraved on the back with '*Va en paix, cher ami'* (Go in peace, dear friend) and I gave him a signed sketch of himself, with '*la tristesse durera toujours'* on the back. 'The sadness will last forever,' reputably Vincent's last words and a lasting testament to my own life.

So it was with a heavy heart two days later that I kissed Marie-Juliette and boarded the train for Paris Gare du Nord and home.

"*La tristesse durera toujours,* Vincent," I whispered as the train pulled away. My eyes filled and I looked away and out of the window so the guard wouldn't see my tears.

Varying Degrees of Nothingness

Looking through my back window,
Back window? Black window…I see,
Varying degrees of nothingness.
The bottom thirds
obscured with rime.
The moon is not my ally.
Pale and insignificant she sits,
Frozen captive in her halo of frost.
A distant row of illuminated windows
hang like a string of pearls.
A beautiful translucence on the
The fat, black collar of the night.
My thoughts turn inward.
The room behind me a host of
Shadows. A conspiracy
Of amorphous nebula, of
No substance…
Still my nerves jangle and mince.

For My Mother

I'll hear your last sigh in the
wind-tormented trees.
I'll hear your last sigh in the new-born cry of future
generations.
I'll hear your last sigh in winter's icy moan and the
sound of summer birdsong.
And when my days are done and a storm rages,
Your last sigh will guide me through the darkness
and into the light.

Soliloquy

What can you possibly want of me? I am bleached and insignificant. Flat as a monotone. An effigy carved in granite. Gentle on the eye, cold to the touch. A tangled mess of contradictions. The grasses whisper to you of my deceit, but still you seek to find that which other women know as fact. That I, in my darkest of days, and in my wintriest of moods will give all but that which is mine, and seek to possess all but that which is offered.

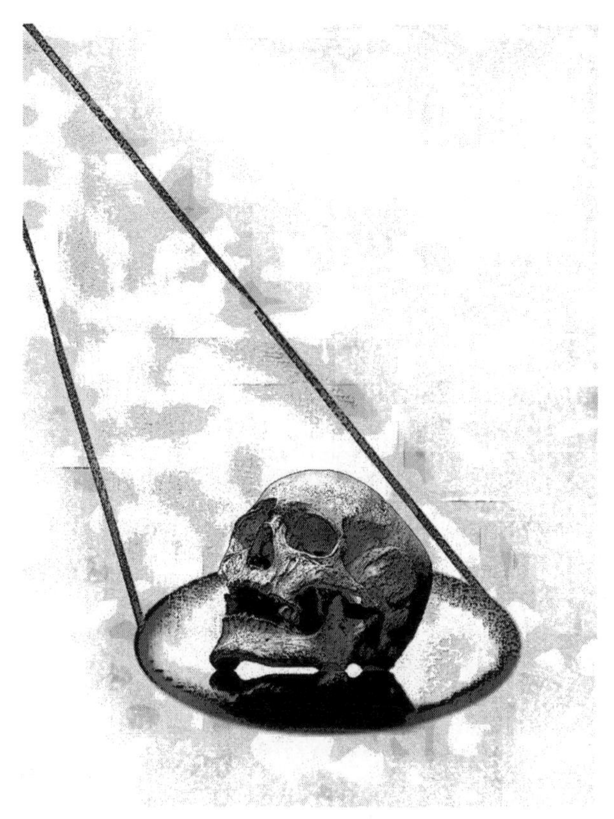

Inspiration For…

'No more trains tonight folks.'

The collective moan from the waiting room hung in the air like a mist.

'What's the meaning of this? My man is waiting with the car at Claring's Brook Halt.' The man who came forward was in his sixties, well-dressed and with a haughty manner that suggested the lower echelons of aristocracy.

'I'm sorry Mr...?'

'Sir! Sir Gregory Harris,' he ventured 'I demand to know…'

'If you would please sit down, Sir.' The stationmaster was in his early fifties, tall, with a pleasant, ruddy face. 'There's a fallen tree on the line at Shearing's Vale, probably the result of the high winds we've been having. I'm afraid no-one's going anywhere tonight.'

Again the stationmaster was greeted by groans and angry murmurings.
'Please, sir, I have to be somewhere.' The girl, who had been previously sat unseen in the

shadowy corner, stepped forward. She was a pretty girl, early twenties. She clutched tightly at her vanity case and coloured when she spoke.

'I'm sorry Madam, but there's no other way out of Little Hubery, unless you walk the ten mile or so to Shearing's Vale, though I heartily advise against it, especially across moorland.'

'Oh!' the girl said quietly and melted back into the shadows.

'But surely man there's a tram…' Sir Gregory again, his face red with exasperation.

'No trams here, Sir. They don't come out this far, and the last trackless left over an hour ago.'

'But that's absurd…'

'I suggest we let the man speak.' The man who stepped forward was in uniform. His rank was low, perhaps that of a Lance Bombardier. Sir Gregory looked around angrily, ready to answer back, but something in the soldier's manner made him think again.

'Thank you, sir,' the stationmaster continued. 'We will have to stay here for the next few hours, until the line has been cleared. Wireless says we're due a mighty storm, but we've plenty of coal for the fire. The refreshment room is closed, but I've tea and Horlicks in my office, if you're not afraid to drink from mugs.'

'Dear God,' said Harris.

'Please, Gregory.' The lady beside him took his arm. She was of a similar age, coiffured and wearing a mink stole.

'I'll ring the other stations on the up line, so if anyone has people waiting, they'll be made aware of the situation. Meanwhile, I'll fetch some more coal and get a good blaze going. I suggest you make yourselves comfortable, least for now.'

The soldier stood up. 'I'll help you,' he said. The stationmaster thanked him and the two men left, the angry mutterings of the other passengers still audible after the waiting room door was closed.

Five people regarded each another in morose silence. The waiting room was full of shades cast by the dimly lit gaslights, but a good fire blazed in the grate and the shadows, bathed in the amber glow, danced wretchedly across the walls and ceiling. A clock ticked sonorously above the mantle, but even that was silenced by the deafening roar of the wind that sped along the hollow, hitting the exposed station building with full force and rattling the ill-fitting windows in their frames.

The stationmaster returned with hot drinks. The rain had begun, a deluge that, caught on the wind's breath, hurled itself at the station windows like a spray of bullets. The soldier flinched at the memories the sound created. The well-to-do couple sat gloomily, arm-in-arm, the occasional grumble coming from Sir about missing a fine dinner and how the weather played havoc with his arthritic leg. The young lady sat back in the shadows as though afraid the light would betray her secrets, and an elderly professor had joined Harris and his wife and was complaining about rail travel in general.

Only the middle-aged man with the greasy hair and sallow skin seemed content with the situation. He made no attempts to talk with the others, merely sat, grinning to himself, a strange, unpleasant smile that unnerved all who looked at him.

The hours passed slowly. The stationmaster had brought the wireless from next door, and the stranded travellers listened to soothing late night music from Woody Herman and Artie Shaw. The late hour had brought them closer to the fire, and they began to make conversation.

The young lady, Charlotte, was on her way to take up the position of history teacher in a school some fifty miles north. The professor, retired, was on his way home after visiting friends. Sir Gregory and Lady Harris were returning from visiting their son in London.

'We thought it would be quicker and more pleasant by train,' growled the old man with some rancour.

The soldier was on leave. Still stationed in Berlin, he was grabbing a few precious days at home with his family.

'And how about you, my friend?' The stationmaster turned to the man sat beside the fire, who had up until now remained silent and aloof.

Suddenly the door opened with a tremendous crash. The fire died and the waiting room was plunged into darkness as the gaslights were blown out by a gust of wind that blew around the room, chilling them to the bone. Everyone jumped with fright. One of the ladies screamed.

'All right ladies and gentlemen. It's only the wind.' The stationmaster shot up and closed the door against the storm. The soldier re-lit the gaslights and the fire flared up once more.

‘Oh!’ exclaimed Charlotte. ‘Where did he go?’ The seat in which the sallow-faced man had been sat was empty.

‘The only way out was through this door,’ said the stationmaster, puzzled. ‘Surely he didn’t have time to leave?’

The others looked at each other, each one overcome by a feeling of dread. The stationmaster looked gravely into the fire.

‘I didn’t want to tell you before. I didn’t want to alarm you…’

‘What is it, man?’ interrupted Harris, his voice unsteady, quavering.
‘The station has a reputation of being haunted, Sir.’

‘Oh come, man,’ cut in the soldier, angrily.

The wind howled around the isolated station, and the travellers sought comfort in the fire and the close proximity of others.

‘The year was nineteen thirty-five. A local man, whom I shall call Joseph, had everything to live for. He had recently become engaged to his childhood sweetheart and there were rumours abound at the bank in which he was clerk that big changes were going to be made. He knew the manager was due to retire and after all his hard work, Joseph was convinced that promotion was a certainty.'

'All went terribly wrong however, when Joseph was called into his manager's office and accused of pilfering from customers' accounts. Just small amounts, hardly noticeable, but when you added them up…well…' The stationmaster looked around at the others sat beside the fire.

'It seemed Joseph wanted to give his love the wedding day she deserved. He was dismissed instantly. A few days later on the eve of his big day, Joe took a bottle of sleeping pills and went and sat on top of the railway bridge, less than a mile away, on the up line.'

He nodded towards the bridge. All was still and hushed in the waiting room.

'It seems he had left a note to his intended, telling her of his dismissal and his shame and apologising for failing her. She had run to the bridge with the intentions of stopping him. She meant to tell him she forgave him and still wanted to be his wife.' The stationmaster hung his head.

'She arrived just in time to see him jump in front of the 7.35 to Harrogate. On impact with the train, his poor, wretched head was severed cleanly from his shoulders.'

Lady Harris shrieked and buried her head in her husband's greatcoat, and four other pairs of eyes turned to the empty chair in the waiting room corner.

Jamie awoke to a hammering on the waiting room door.

'C'mon J, we've got to be going.'

He groaned and turned over in his sleeping bag. The light stole into the darkened room as his friend's grinning face appeared at the door.'

'Still alive then,' he said as he kicked the sleeping bag.

'Oi!' Jamie retorted.

'I guess you picked the right night for it mate, storm an' all,' his friend said, throwing a fiver on the floor. 'You win. You spent a night alone in the haunted station.'

Jamie said nothing as he rolled his sleeping bag and pocketed the note. He made his way outside and mounted the bike he'd left tied to tree. He was already pedalling away when his friend jumped on his own bike and caught him up.

'So d'ya sees anything, J? Any ghosts?' he asked with a mocking sideways glance.

'Naw,' said Jamie. 'Cept, I felt as though I wasn't alone, an' I kep' hearing this weird old music…'

A Strange Encounter at
Little Hubery

I

I am the stranger in the mist.
The breeze that stirs the leafless bough.
The blood-red sky, a sunset gift.
The cold north wind that brings the snow.

I am the whisper in the class
The writing on the playground wall
The tales around the campfire late
The footsteps in the empty hall

I am the challenge to which you rise
The dreams that fade within your hands
Lain waste as land when wind doth blow
And trickle through fingers like grains of sand.

Jacob's Plight

Jacob stared blankly at the camera, as if afraid his soul would be lost, forever trapped inside the image, immortalised. Behind him a wooden dorm building, peeling paint, windowless and with a rusty corrugated roof. To his left a line of captives waiting to be branded and photographed, their hair shorn, their bellies hungry and their eyes dead. Children huddled close to mothers, who were as lost and afraid as they were. Elsewhere it was a warm spring day on this May afternoon of '43, but the birds didn't sing much around here.

A row of armed guards stood behind the photographer, on their armbands the symbol of evil that struck fear into the hearts of so many.

"Smile, you filthy Jew," spat one of the guards. The boy looked at him, dazed and bewildered, and a huge flat hand reached over and slapped him hard across the face.

“Zat vill put some colour in his cheeks, za little bastard.” The other guards laughed, and Jacob managed a forced but feeble smile as he held back the tears.

Mustn’t cry, Jacob told himself. Yesterday a little girl who wouldn’t stop crying was gunned down where she stood, the Nazis not caring who else got caught in the crossfire.

The shutter closed on the camera, the flash temporarily blinding the boy.

In the letters they were told to write to their families, letters which accompanied the propaganda shots, the Jews were given ten minutes to inform those back home how good they were being treated in the camp and how fair the Nazis were. In the hut next to theirs, their men folk were being rounded up, ready for the shower block.

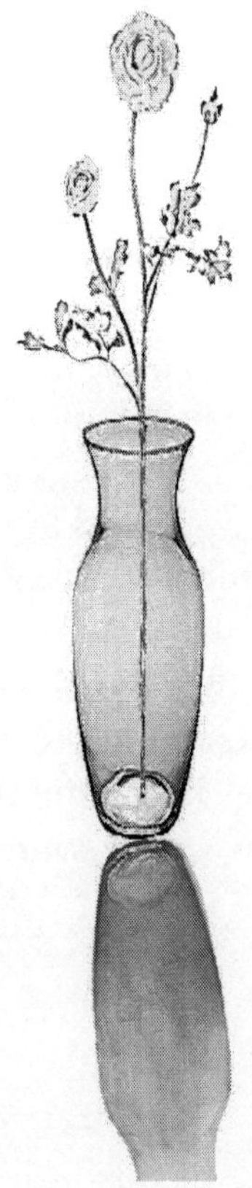

Inanimate Musings

Perhaps,
The thing to be
If I wasn't a vase
In the window, is
An aeroplane wing
Soaring to great
Heights…

And seeing from
A bird's eye view,
The world beneath
The cotton wool clouds.

I'd glide upon the
Ether like an eagle, and
Feel the warm currents of
Air on my underbelly

That's the thing with
Being a vase on a window sill,
You see.
While one eye is sentinel to
The goings on in the home,
The other observes with
Wonderment and longing, the
World behind its glass confine.

For Jessica

My world is velvet, like a purr. It is a world of luxury and comfort. Of hot afternoons full of sweet dreams and salmon whiskers.

Sometimes my world is shadows, as I wait patiently in dark places, biding my time, crouched and waiting to pounce, to strike, to tease, to kill…some beast I have absolutely no intention of eating.

My world is a fur rug and a blazing fire, whose warmth and dreamy amber curl I show my appreciation of with the occasional opening of an eye.

My world is my bed, cushion soft and smelling of the garden. It is a space that I, in my more generous of moods, may share with another of my kind, and sometimes…even with my human.

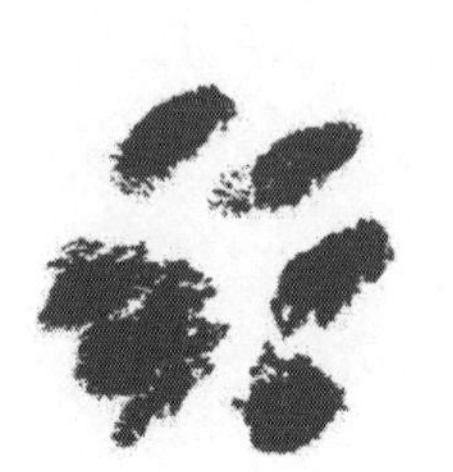

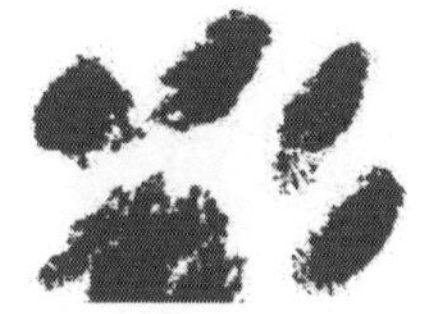

Memories are…

…but reminders of the things that happen in our lives, that make us who we are. Without them we would live our lives in rotation, repeating past mistakes time and time again, like the moth who returns to the candle flame that only moments ago burnt its wings. Some memories scar and that scar remains, fading in time to that dull but constant ache we learn to live with. Years later, we recall these memories with sadness. Something, perhaps a whisper on the breeze, or the perfume of a stranger who shares your carriage on a train, reawakens within us memories we thought were lost to us forever. But some memories are best kept hidden. For the present is but a slave to the past and takes its direction from a path already trodden.

Haunted

Ghost words hang in the air
Like balloons. Things
Of no substance.
I try to pluck them
To hold them in my hands.
Still they evade capture

Just bubbles blown
Through a hoop, melting
Away in my palm, like dreams
That faded and died, leaving me
Silent and devoid. Caught
Between worlds.

Neome

She knew the night her fiancé died that they would still go ahead with the wedding, as was her people's custom. Silently and without fuss, she prepared herself for her forthcoming nuptials.

She chose a dress of ivory silk and a bouquet of cream roses and calla. Her cheeks were allowed a discreet blush. Her raven hair hung in ringlets and her lips were painted with beeswax stained with the juice of berries.

When they came for her, she followed them out and through the flower-strewn streets, oblivious to the wide-eyed awe of bare-footed village children and the whispers and mocking grins of the fish-wives.

The moon hid her pity behind a cloudy veil sheer as the bride's own, as she lay garter-thighed beside her husband in the dark mausoleum of their wedding bed, and as the stone closed above her, she kissed the stars goodbye.

The Soldier's Return
(For my Grandad Jack Phillips, who never came home.)

Sunset on the lane and the trees huddle, a silent conspiracy, silhouetted against a darkening sky streaked with crimson. The wood-burners lie idle tonight. The mild air belies the naivety of the season, and the nightingale on her branch sings as sweetly now as any midsummer's eve. In the nearby fields, huge clods of freshly dug black earth sit motionless as hunchback rats, snouting for food amongst remains in the gutter.

I approach the inn to sounds of those making merry within its warm familiar keep, and imagine I hear with a lightening of heart the laughter of patrons long since deceased. Their conversations dimmed with the passing of time, but an echo of them remains, for their laughter is absorbed over the years by the lime-lined, crumbling, pitted walls of the old public house. Past chocolate-box cottages and into the village, there church bells peal joyously, welcoming the prodigal home from distant war-torn lands.

The sun is low, bowing its graceful head as if to whisper 'sweet dreams' to an earth that grows ever darker in its absence. From all around, midges dart restlessly on the fragrant spring breeze, as if afraid to land on a blazing earth's crust.

I am lulled by a far-off droning from the bee keeper's garden and the thought of home now only minutes away. How I have dreamed of this and kept those dreams close to my heart. They kept me warm through the bitter winter of my war days and the oh-so-lonely nights far from my beloved Beatrice.

From an open cottage window, the smell of fresh bread lingers on the warm, still air, awakening memories of a pre-war life, and I feel as I have a thousand times before, a stirring deep inside, a feeling of hope and expectation tinged with the purple hues of sadness.

Dusk on the lane and the sun is absent, as though the conspirator trees have blocked out its rays with their coming together of branches. The impending night has a mild air about it. Everything is hushed into an almost stillness, the day's creatures ready to retire, the nocturnal beasts not yet stirred from their slumber. The village children, despite laments and pleas to the contrary, have all been rounded up and herded indoors for supper. They are not alone in their protestations, for the gate of the old cottage creaks and groans when challenged, and the old homestead greets with a suspiciously dejected air, an air almost of neglect, and seems to stare with cold, unseeing eyes, as if at an intruder trying to violate its boundaries. The latch on the old stable door adds to the feeling of decay, its glossy, black, shiny paint eaten away by rust.

The cottage is empty! Two years' worth of dust lies undisturbed on the mantle, and shadows scurry into corners as the door opens. From the garden comes the chirruping of crickets in the hedge, and a dormouse wanders in somewhat boldly and disappears into a hole in the skirting. I light an old oil lamp, discarded on the mantle, one of the few remaining relics of my life here. In its melancholy glow I cast no shadow.

Spiders, surprised by the light, flee into the dark sanctum of the corner. The lamplight grows dim and the room grows cold. Outside, all is suddenly still and quiet, but for a distant heartbeat that fades with every pulse…a silent tear, somewhere falls, and the whispering grasses in the nearby meadow tell me,

I am home.
I am home.
I am home…

Lance Bombardier Jack Phillips
Royal Artillery

Turn the Page
For Other Offerings
From
Jack C. Phillips
and
Camelot Publishing Company

A Strange Encounter at Little Hubery
By Jack. C. Phillips

Seven strangers are trapped in a remote and lonely railway station on the desolate Yorkshire moors when a freak storm brings a tree down on the tracks. As railway staff battle to clear the line further north, it becomes apparent that those stranded will be there for the night, and they reluctantly settle down in the waiting room as the storm rages about the exposed moorland.

Who lurks in the dimly lit station, watching the passengers as they huddle around the fire? And what lies in wait for them outside on the storm-tossed moor? One by one, stories are told and secret revealed, and it soon becomes unnervingly evident to those seeking sanctuary at the old station that things at Little Hubery are not what they seem.

A real spine-tingler to curl up with beneath the duvet on a cold winter's night.

No. 41 Burlington Road
By Jack. C. Phillips

When his wife suddenly up and leaves him without warning, Jared Colne is left severely depressed and agoraphobic and cuts himself off from his friends and family. Having no contact with the outside world and dependent upon alcohol and anti-depressants to get him through the day, Jared begins spying on his neighbours on Burlington Road, and soon finds himself living in a dark, fantasy world where nothing is as it seems. As things quickly spiral out of control, Jared realises it's not only his sanity he's in danger of losing.

Who is the pale-faced boy who watches him from beneath the lamp-post across the road? Who lurks in the shadows in the abandoned house opposite? Where does his neighbour Graham go at the dead of night? And who or what is haunting his home, filling his lonely, sleepless nights with fear and dread?

With just the right amounts of comic relief, passion, tears and creepy, tense moments, Burlington Road crosses many genres and is guaranteed to keep you hooked until the story's gripping climax.

Tales of the Mysterious and Macabre
By Simon Parker

Ever wonder what makes a serial killer take those first tentative steps? Or what you'd feel if a pile of rotting flesh grabbed you with putrid fingers? How psychotic would you become if you discovered hell was a real place and you were in it? Find the inky places between the shadows in these tales of psychological terror and darkest fantasy that bring the gothic tradition bang up to date.

Released April of 2016

Heart Songs
By Mica Rossi

Our feelings change hour by hour. Anger, love, regret, fear, joy, envy, despair or compassion, we have all known them intimately. Whether internal or circumstantial, our lives can be completely transformed by the emotional climates we experience.

The stories and poems in Mica Rossi's *Heart Songs* are about the emotional curves in our journeys, the unexpected just as we're traveling the smoothest of roads or find ourselves in a dark place we can't escape. They are a three hundred sixty degree look at the music to which we dance and the heart songs we sing.

Available now from Camelot Publishing Company on Amazon everywhere

16837206R00096

Printed in Great Britain
by Amazon